MYCENAE

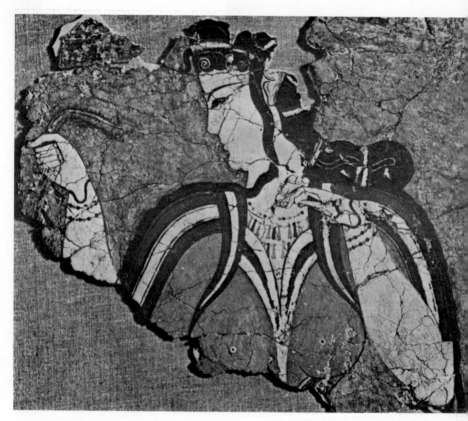

The «Mycenaean Lady» fresco

GEORGE E. MYLONAS
Director of the Excavations of Mycenae

MYCENAE
A GUIDE TO ITS RUINS
AND
ITS HISTORY

SIXTH EDITION

ATHENS 1977

TO THE MEMORY

OF

HEINRICH SCHLIEMANN

PANAGHIOTES STAMATAKES

CHRESTOS TSOUNTAS

DIMITRIOS EVANGELIDES

ANTONIOS KERAMOPOULLOS

ALAN J. B. WACE

GEORG KARO

IOANNES PAPADIMITRIOU

NIKOLAOS VERDELES

SERAPHIM CHARITONIDES

Who devoted a small or a greater part of their lives to the study and excavation of Mycenae this small volume is reverently dedicated.

MYCENAEAN CHRONOLOGY

Mycenaean Age ca. 1600 - 1120 B.C.
Sub - periods:
Mycenaean (or Late Helladic) I   ca. 1600 - 1500 B.C.
Mycenaean (or Late Helladic) II   ca. 1500 - 1400 B.C.
        Mycenaean (or Late Helladic) III (Mycenaean period par excellence)

III A.	ca. 1400 - 1300 B.C.
III B.	ca. 1300 - 1190 B.C.
III C.	ca. 1190 - 1120 B.C.

SELECTED BIBLIOGRAPHY

MARINATOS, S. and HIRMER, M., Crete and Mycenae, London 1960.
MYLONAS, G.E., Mycenae and the Mycenaean Age, Princeton 1966.
TSOUNTAS, C. and MANATT, J., The Mycenaean Age, London 1897.
WACE, A.J.B., Mycenae, Princeton 1949.

PREFACE

Thirty years of excavating have brought about the need for a *Guide book* such as this, which contains the latest results of the archaeologists' work. The illustrations and the many plans it contains will, I hope, make easy the study of the ruins which at first glance seem labyrinthine. In Part I of the *Guide* I give a full description of the remains in the acropolis of Mycenae; in Part II an account of the tombs and houses to be found outside the acropolis. In Part III, I offer a concise account of the history and legends of Mycenae, of the excavations and the excavators whose work has made possible the study of the Mycenaean civilization. In this way a rounded picture of the site and its historic role in the affairs of Greece may be obtained from the reading of the *Guide* and the inspection of the site.

In Figure 1 and by means of arrows I suggest the route the visitor should follow in his visit and by means of stars the points from which better views of the ruins and landscapes can be obtained and from which photographs can be taken. Those who intend to visit the subterranean cistern in the northeast corner of the acropolis, one of the most remarkable engineering achievements of the age, should equip themselves with a light torch, necessary also for the inspection of the side chamber of the «Treasury of Atreus».

It is hoped that the visit to the City of Agamemnon will prove a memorable experience for the reader.

GEORGE E. MYLONAS

PART I

THE ACROPOLIS OF MYCENAE

Mycenae is one of the few ancient sites that was never forgotten by man in the course of time. And this because the exploits of one of its kings became the theme of a great epic poem compiled by Homer, the oldest and one of the greatest bards of our Western World. In the *Iliad* we read today, as thousands before us read, that Agamemnon, the king of Mycenae, led a Greek expeditionary force against Troy where Paris, the son of King Priam, had taken the beautiful Helen, wife of Menelaos King of Sparta. The evils that befell the House of Atreus became the themes used by the famous playwrights of Classical Athens. Their immortal tragedies became the teachers of the world, but at the same time the proclaimers of the glory of Mycenae. And when, in 1876, Heinrich Schliemann disclosed the Royal Graves of Mycenae with their treasures, Mycenae once more became the center of interest for the scholar and the layman alike. In the *Iliad* Agamemnon is called the *«Anax of Men»* and the most kingly of the leaders of the Achaeans. Excavations have proved that Mycenae held a preeminent place among the States which participated in the Trojan War, among the States of the Heroic Age of the mainland of Greece, of the Late Bronze Age.

That Age, from ca. 1600 to 1120 B.C., was the most brilliant and prosperous period of Mycenae. Although its hill was inhabited in the Early Bronze Age, from ca. 2500 B.C. on, and perhaps even in the Stone Age, nevertheless tradition maintained that Perseus, the son of Zeus and Danaë, was the Founder of Mycenae and its first king. It is stated that, in the first half of the

14th century B.C., he built its fortification walls using for the task the legendary Cyclopes. Mycenae enjoyed years of prosperity and greatness in the reign of Atreus, ca. 1250 B.C., and even in the years of his son Agamemnon, ca. 1220 to 1190 B.C., who led the Achaeans against Troy. Mycenae is reported by tradition to have been destroyed finally by the Dorians towards the end of the 12th century B.C.

Its ruins, long buried under deep layers of earth, were revealed by a series of Greek and Foreign Scholars — whose names are recorded in the dedication — but it seems that its soil still contains ruins and treasures which systematic research is endeavoring to reveal under the auspices of the Greek Archaeological Society of Athens. In Part III of this study, I give fuller details of the legends, the history and the excavations and to that part I refer the visitor who will have the leisure to read and, hopefylly, to enjoy them.

THE FORTIFICATION WALLS

The hill of Mycenae rises to a top strongly defined by ancient terraces 280 m. (912 feet) above sea level. To the south it is separated from Mt. Zara by a deep ravine known as the Chavos. Its slopes are surrounded by fortification walls which transform it into an acropolis, a citadel roughly triangular in shape encompassing some 30,000 square meters of uneven ground (Figs. 1 and 2). The walls are in the main constructed of roughly shaped stones piled on each other. They are of so large dimensions that the ancient Greeks maintained that only the Cyclopes, with superhuman powers, could have moved and placed them in position. Thence they called them Cyclopean walls and the type of construction they represent even today is known as Cyclopean. The north side of the circuit is the best preserved example of this type of construction. The thickness of the walls ranges from 5.50 to 7.50 m. Their original height is nowhere preserved, but it is figured out that it approached 12 m. The best preserved section, to the south of the Lion Gate, rises 8.25 m. above the rock. The main entrance to the citadel, known as the Lion Gate, is in its northwest corner. The visit to Mycenae usually begins at the gate.

As we follow the road leading to the gate from the modern guardroom where the entrance tickets are sold (Fig. 32a), we have before us the restored northwest corner of the circuit wall, a formidable stone construction built on the rocky slope (Fig. 3). Perhaps we could stop here and recall that this was built in the Late Bronze Age, when an enemy who might attack the citadel would be armed only with swords, spears, bows and arrows, slings and sling-bullets. We may well wonder how with such

Fig. 2. Air view of the Citadel from the West
(Photograph by courtesy of the Greek Airforce)

weapons in bronze they could have hoped to storm the citadel. Evidently only through treachery or a long siege the surrender of the defenders could be obtained. Now we can realize why it took the Achaeans so long to capture Troy, since that city was a citadel similar to that of Mycenae.

The difficulties of storming the citadel were increased by the way in which its main entrance was designed. In front of the Lion Gate we find a narrow court some 15 meters in length and 7.25 meters in width (Fig. 32 No. 1). This court forced the reduction in number of an attacking enemy and thus weakened the effort. Furthermore, the court is flanked by heavy walls. On its east side and for quite a distance rises a formidable wall, while a bastion occupies its west side (Fig. 32 No. 2). Defenders on the bastion could strike the undefended right side of soldiers advancing against the gate, while those on the east wall would force them to keep their shields in the normal position over the left shoulder. The stones employed for the construction of the east wall of the bastion, and of the Lion Gate are conglomerate that abounds in the neighborhood. The conglomerate blocks are hammer-dressed, more or less rectangular in shape but of different heights and are placed almost in horizontal courses in a quasi-ashlar type of masonry (Fig. 4); in the regular ashlar construction all courses are of equal height. While the bastion is built solidly of conglomerate, the east wall is formed of a single outer row of conglomerate blocks masking the core of an older Cyclopean wall. It as well as the bastion and the Lion Gate are later additions to an original citadel wall that was built of limestone in the Cyclopean style about 1340 B.C. The east masking wall, the bastion, and the Lion Gate date from about 1250 B.C.

Perhaps we should note that some of the conglomerate blocks have very large dimensions; for example, note the third block from the corner of the bastion on the ground level. The same is true for the blocks of the Cyclopean construction. We may well wonder how such blocks were lifted to their position. No traces are to be seen on the stones indicating the use of hoisting machinery and it is generally assumed that the masons used inclines or ramps of earth over which the blocks were pushed and pulled to position. When the walls were finished the ramps were removed. We may also note that in the northwest corner of the bastion a different style of masonry is preserved or restored. It is known as the polygonal style. It dates from the third century B.C. and it is a repair of a breach in the conglomerate and Cyclopean walls that seems to have been made in the destruction of 468 B.C.

THE LION GATE (Figures 4 and 32 No. 3).

The main entrance to the citadel is a truly megalithic monument. Four large conglomerate blocks were used for its construction and they were fashioned to shape by hammer and saw. The gate is almost as wide as high, measuring 3.10 m. in height and 2.95 m. in width at the threshold and 2.78 m. in width below

Fig. 3. Restored Northwest Corner of the Citadel of Mycenae

the lintel. Thus it narrows slightly upwards. Its threshold, a monolith 4.65 m. in length, 2.31 m. in width and 0.88 m. in maximum thickness, cracked in Mycenaean times under the stress of the weight.

On its surface are apparent traces of its life and use. Along either side we find shallow depressions, two on the east, one on the west side, which until recently were taken to have been made by the wheels of chariots or cart wheels. It is now maintained with reason that all the cuttings on the threshold date from the third century B.C. and that the shallow depressions were drains. The opening of the gate was closed by a double door of wood decorated on the outside with bronze ornaments. Each of the sections of the door was fastened to a vertical beam acting as a pivot and around that beam the doors revolved: the ends of the beam projecting above and below the door were fitted in pivot holes in the threshold and the lintel; the pivot holes on the lintel are well preserved. Those on the threshold were altered in modern times. On the inner face of the doorjamb we have rectangular sockets, one on each side, made to receive a bar or crossbeam that secured the door when closed. We also have on each doorjamb oblong recesses in which the door handles could sink when it was desired to keep the door wide open.

These doorjambs are large monoliths of conglomerate worked by saw and hammer measuring 3.10 m. in height, 1.74 m. in width and 0.54 m. in thickness at the inner end, while at the façade their width amounts to 0.66 m. Their rebate served to accomodate the vertical beams that acted as pivots to the doors. The doorjambs supported the lintel, a monolith of conglomerate, some 4.50 m. in length, 1.98 m. in width and 0.80 m. maximum height at the center. It is estimated that it weighs some 18 tons. Over the lintel the wall construction presents an interesting feature, characteristic of late Mycenaean architecture — the blocks of the wall are so placed that each projects a little beyond the one below it, so that an empty triangular space over the lintel results. This method of placing stones to span a distance is known as corbel

Fig. 4. The Lion Gate

vaulting, and the empty triangle of space is known as the relieving triangle, for the purpose of the arrangement is to relieve the lintel from the weight of a heavy wall above it that may bring about a break in the lintel with disastrous results. The relieving triangle of our gate, however, is blocked by a large, roughly triangular slab of hard limestone some 3.30 m. in height, 3.90 m. in width at its broadest point, and 0.70 m. in thickness. It is actually supported only at the two ends of its base and thus its weight is diverted to the sides and to the doorposts.

The relief carved on the slab is the oldest really monumental piece of sculpture of our Western World and has given the name to the gate: Lion Gate. On either side of a column of the Minoan type —wider at the top than at the bottom— bearing an entablature stands a lion with its front paws on altars on which the column is based. The heads of the lions, made of different, softer material and attached to the slab by dowels whose dowel-holes are apparent, have been lost. It was stated in the past that the heads were of bronze perhaps gilt, but scholars now believe that they were made of steatite, a soft stone more conducive than limestone to carving elaborate details. The heads were rendered full front and faced the visitor as he approached the gate. The vigorous modeling of the animals and the sense of structure and proportion give the relief life and an air of dignity seldom surpassed in prehistoric art. Its successful adaptation to the triangle above the lintel makes it one of the most successful architectural reliefs of all times.

Scholars have not reached unanimity as to the interpretation of the composition. One thing is clear; since the column supports a symbolic representation of a roof structure it cannot stand for a divinity as was believed in the past. It symbolizes a structure guarded by the lions. That structure can only be the royal palace on the summit of the citadel; the royal palace standing for the ruling family that dwells in it. The lions are the emblem of Mycenae, and they are guarding the royal family, the royal dynasty of Mycenae. The altars from which the column rises express the belief that the right of the house and dynasty to rule is given from the gods — it indicates the divine right of the king, known to have existed in Greece of the Heroic Era from the *Iliad* of Homer. If this interpretation is correct, and I believe it is, then we have to accept the view that the relief is the *coat of arms* of the royal house of Mycenae, the oldest coat of arms in the history of our Western World. The relief and the gate were made around 1250 B.C. According to the tradition, the legendary genealogies, and the possible estimate of time from archaeological evidence, the king who ruled over Mycenae at that time was Atreus the father of Agamemnon. The relief over the gate, then, is the coat of arms of the house of Agamemnon. Whether we accept this view or not (and I do hold it) the fact remains that the relief was standing in its position when Agamemnon marshalled his troops through the gate to lead them against Troy.

16

The date of the Lion Gate, ca. 1250 B.C., will lead us to the consideration of the various periods of the walls of Mycenae. Recent excavations prove that the fortification walls are not of one period, but that the area surrounded by them was gradually increased in well established stages. The oldest fortification walls that survived are of the Cyclopean type and date to about 1340 B.C. They enclosed a smaller area than later, whose west side was closed by a wall that began at the existing northwest corner, went straight beyond the area of the Lion Gate and continued to the ravine known as the Chavos (Fig. 5:1). Then the Lion Gate did not exist and its area and that of its court and Grave Circle A were outside the fortified citadel.

Around 1250 B.C. the Mycenaeans decided to enlarge the area of the citadel to the west and south. Then they built the Lion Gate and the west Cyclopean wall that begins at the Lion Gate and in a graceful curve sweeps around the Grave Circle that was now brought within the citadel (Fig. 5:2). The older wall of the west side of the first citadel was then demolished. Towards the end of the 13th century an addition was made at the northeast end of the citadel to accomodate the underground cistern to be visited later (Fig. 5:3).

AREA OF THE INNER COURT (Figure 32 No. 4).

Now let us enter the citadel. As we cross the threshold we find ourselves in a little court flanked by walls in conglomerate some 4 meters square. Originally the court was covered and perhaps by means of its roof the top of the walls was reached. On the lefthand side, or the east side, there is a small chamber some 4 meters in length, 1.30 m. in width, and 1.50 m. in extreme height, whose function remains uncertain. Some propose here a room for the guards of the gate, others suggest that it housed watchdogs, and still others consider it a shrine. The area beyond the court was dug away by Schliemann and so few remains survive. But we may note to the east a strong wall (Fig. 32 No. 6) that supported a

17

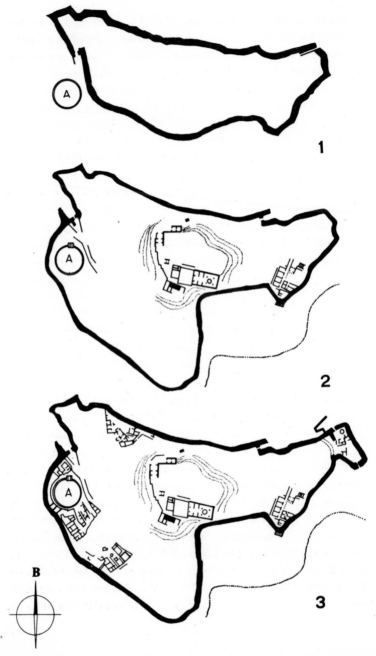

Fig. 5. Three Stages in the Development of the Circuit Walls. A, Grave Circle.
B, North

terrace by means of which the top of the walls was reached. Similarly behind the west wall of the court are to be seen scanty remains of walls that indicate the existence of a staircase which led also to the top of the walls (Fig. 32 No. 5). In front and in the distance is the great ramp that led to the palace on the summit.

Before we reach the ramp we may note the numerous foundations on the right - hand side, the west. They are the foundations of corridors and rooms built against the west Cyclopean wall (Fig. 32 No. 7). Possibly the building originally stood two stories above the basement. It is now known as the Granary since a small quantity of carbonized remains of vetches, wheat, and barley was found stored in vessels that stood in the basement at the time of the excavation. The dimensions of the building perhaps indicate that it served also as a guard house of soldiers responsible for the defense of the gate. In its latest form it lasted to the very end of the Mycenaean period and was finally destroyed by fire in the great catastrophe of ca. 1120 B.C.

GRAVE CIRCLE A (Figures 6 and 33).

To the south of the «Granary and Guard House», or on the right - hand side as we proceed towards the ramp, we find Grave Circle A, the royal cemetery explored by Schliemann in 1876. It is a circular area some 28 meters in diameter enclosed by a low parapet wall made of two parallel rows of shelly or plain sandstone slabs set vertically at a distance of 1.35 meters from each other. At the top horizontally placed slabs closed the opening (one such slab is in place at the beginning of the circle beyond the doorposts) while the distance between the slabs was filled with earth. Thus a solid parapet wall, 0.90 to 1.50 m. in height, was formed, of a striking appearance. One enters the Circle through its opening on the north side constructed like the rest of the parapet, of a double row of slabs, with elaborate doorposts projecting north and south beyond the sides. (Schliemann believed that these doorposts were cisterns). The threshold is made of

19

Fig. 6. General View. Grave Circle A. The Argive Plain in the Distance

three large slabs and along the east side of the Circle the area was paved with slabs.

Within this area Schliemann found and explored 5 shaft graves (Nos. I-V). After his departure Stamatakes discovered a sixth grave, No. VI (Fig. 33). These shaft graves are mere rectangular trenches cut through the earth and the soft rock under it. They vary in size and depth: the smallest measures 3.00 by 3.50 m. and the largest 4.50 by 6.40 m. the depth varies from 1 to 3 or 4 meters. The sides of the shafts are lined with narrow rubble walls that rise from the floor to a height ranging from 0.75 to 1.50 m. On the rubble walls rested wooden beams placed across the width of the grave at short distance from each other to support a roof structure made of stone slabs or thatch. Thus over the floor a cavity was formed and on the floor, covered with pebbles, the bodies of the dead were placed. The roof of slabs or thatch was covered with a thick layer of clay to seal the grave against seepage of moisture.

Over it earth was poured until the surface of the slope was reached. Then a funeral meal was consumed in honor of the dead; its remains — bones of animals or sea-shells — were covered with earth until a small mound was formed. On top of the mound was erected a stele, that is, a flat slab of stone one face of which was sometimes covered with relief. When a relative was to be buried in the same grave, the stele, the earth, and the roof structure would be removed and the body be laid to rest next to the kinsman who had been buried earlier. The roof would again be constructed, the shaft above it would be filled with earth, the funeral meal would be held, then would follow the raising of the mound of earth and the placing of the stele. This process was repeated as many times as it was necessary to use the grave. All burials were inhumations and evidently cremation was not practiced at the time. Schliemann reported one case of embalming which has remained unique.

Fig. 7.
Grave Circle A.
Gold Mask from
Grave V.
So-called Mask
of Agamemnon

Within the six shaft graves 19 skeletons were found, 8 belonging to men, 9 to women, and 2 to children. Evidently they were laid in the graves in their fineries and many gifts and furnishings, including vases containing supplies, were placed along side and in the corners of the grave. It is not the purpose here to describe or discuss the objects found by Schliemann and Stamatakes in these shaft graves; these are exhibited and can be seen in the Mycenaean Room of the National Archaeological Museum of Athens. But we should note that among them were bronze swords and daggers, some with engraved or inlaid decoration, goblets and cups in gold and silver, five masks of gold, more than 850 discs of goldleaf some 6 cm. in diameter, bearing elaborate designs in repoussé work and used for the decoration of garments, diadems and armbands in gold with delicately executed embossed patterns, cross-rosettes of gold, rhytons of gold and of silver (one in the form of a bull's head in silver decked with gold, another in gold in the form of a lion head) rings and gems, necklaces and amber beads. Schliemann states that the objects of gold he found weigh 14 kilograms. The wealth and artistry of these objects astounded the world and still excite the admiration of the visitor and the student.

At the time of the discovery Schliemann believed that he had found the graves of Agamemnon and of those who were murdered with him; the graves mentioned by Pausanias. Indeed, one of the gold masks he identified as the mask of Agamemnon and often enough it is called by that name even today (Fig. 7). And so when he cleared the fifth grave Schliemann stopped digging; he reasoned that «Pausanias mentions five graves. I have found them. No longer is it necessary to excavate further». After his departure, Stamatakes, the official representative of the Greek Ar chaeological Society at the excavations, discovered and cleared the VIth shaft grave. Soon after Schliemann, however, scholars proved that the shaft graves of Circle A belong to a period removed some three and a half centuries from the days of Agamemnon. The graves belong to the family that ruled Mycenae

22

from about 1580 to 1510 B.C. Who that family was, what were the names of its members, we do not know and we cannot even guess; we are sure, however, that they were Greek-speaking Indo Europeans. Schliemann's exploration of Grave Circle A can be considered as one of the most important archaeological discoveries in the Greek world.

Beyond the south side of Grave Circle A, and along the west Cyclopean wall we have the foundations of a number of houses known under a variety of names (Figure 33 E, Z, H). Beyond these houses in the last five years was revealed the Cult Center of Mycenae, whose area is not as yet open to visitors.

THE GREAT RAMP AND THE CULT CENTER
(Figures 33 Γ and 34).

Over the east side of Grave Circle A towers a massive Cyclopean wall that retains the great ramp. Leaving the circle by its entrance-way (Fig. 33 A) we can reach the preserved part of the ramp by means of a narrow stairway in concrete made in modern times for the convenience of the visitors. To the left of the ramp (Fig. 33 Δ) there is a large cistern, constructed against the rock of the hill part of which was dug away to accomodate it. The cistern dates from the third century B.C. from the years when the citadel was transformed into a township by the Argives. Its original watertight plaster still adheres to the sides.

The ramp, that in its present form dates from the last quarter of the 13th century B.C., ranges in width from 4.10 to 5.75 meters and is preserved to a length of 24 meters. Its original surface was removed in many places by archaeologists who investigated its fill and then replaced it, but apparently in antiquity it was paved with cobble stones. At its south end it breaks abruptly and it seems that at about that line originally it turned at right angles to the east to continue its ascent to the summit. The south end of the Ramp, towering above the Grave Circle (Figure 33*), affords an

23

excellent vantage point for a general view and for photography, of the Circle, the west Cyclopean Wall, and the foundations of the houses between them.

Beyond the break of the Ramp to the south, the existing foundations of four rooms belong to a third century B.C. building believed to have been used as an oil and wine press. Farther to the south from the building the visitor could reach a point (indicated in Figure 1 S) below which a good view from above could be obtained of the Cult Center of Mycenae. The interesting area of the Cult Center includes a basement room (Figure 34 T) with a loft where a number of clay statuettes were found. The peculiar nature of these statuettes becomes clear from the specimen illustrated in Figure 30. To the west of the basement a «shrine» was revealed (Figure 34 T 2) with frescoes, now exhibited in the Museum at Nafplion, where also are to be seen the statuettes from the loft and other recent finds from the citadel. In the summer of 1972 was revealed a round altar, perhaps the great altar of Mycenae, to the south of the frescoed shrine (Figure 34 K). Above this lies the well-known «Tsountas House» (Figure 34 A). To the northeast of the «House of Tsountas», and at a higher level, were brought to light a shrine with a horseshoe shaped altar and a slaughtering stone for the sacrificial animals (No. Γ) and before its north entrance a rectangular altar (No. Δ). To the shrine and altars led a long «processional way» (No. B, B), which was reached from the palace through a monumental stairway and doorway. To the southwest a large building has been cleared, which, perhaps, served as the dwelling place of the high priest of Mycenae and the personnel of the Cult Center. It was decorated with wonderful frescoes, fragments of which have survived. Among these are the famous «Mycenaean Lady», and representations of figure-eight shields. The buildings with the frescoes and the shrines, forming the Cult Center of Mycenae, seem to have been destroyed at the end of the 13th century B.C. Rebuilt then partially, continued to be in use to the end of the 12th century B.C., when the final destruction of the site took place.

24

ASCENT TO THE SUMMIT (Figure 8).

It is generally believed that from its existing south end the ramp, or the avenue which formed its continuation, turned at right angles to the east, proceeded for some 30 meters up the western slope of the hill and then, in the closing years of the Mycenaean Age, forked in two directions. One of the branches (Fig. 8 Γ) gradually ascended the slope in a northeasterly direction and through the north stairway led to the northwestern grand entrance of the palace. The eastern end of that branch has recently been discovered and part of it is now being used by the visitors returning from the Postern Gate of the citadel. The other branch (Fig. 8 E) proceeded in a southeasterly direction to terminate at a stairway known as the grand stairway, that was added to the southwest corner of the palace in the last years of its use. The visitors today follow a modern path (marked by a double dotted line in Figure 8) leading straight to the top and ascending a final stairway, made in modern times, reach the small outer court in front of the northwestern entrance of the palace (Fig. 8 P).

THE PALACE ON THE SUMMIT (Figures 8 and 35).

The northwest entrance is in the form of a propylon with a roofed monostyle outer portico facing the north and a second inner roofed portico with one column on its axis facing the interior, the south (Fig. 35 No. 1). Between the two porticoes was the doorway that has not survived. The bases of the columns were restored in their positions which were determined accurately from their foundation walls. Before one enters the propylon it will be instructive to go around the northwest corner of the palace (Fig. 35 No. 2) to note the foundations of two rooms preserved below the high retaining wall of the summit terrace (from the third century B.C.). These rooms served the palace guards who controlled the ramp used by the visitors to the palace who came up the north stairway. A few steps of that stairway can be seen

25

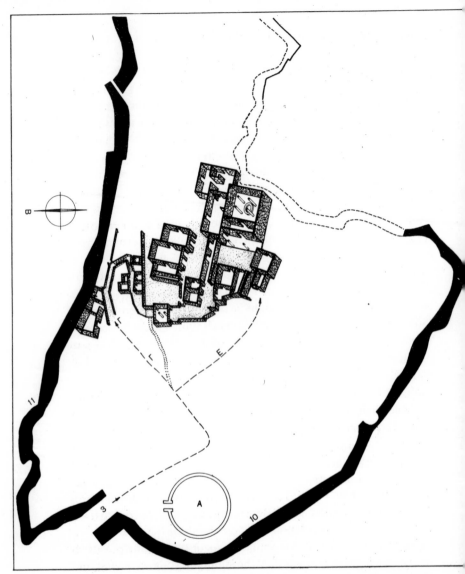

Fig. 8. Ascent to the Summit and the Palace. A, Grave Circle. 3, Lion Gate. 10,
West Cyclopean Wall. 11, North Cyclopean Wall. Γ, Road to the Northeast. S,
Northeast stairway. E, Road to the Southwest Staircase. P, grand entrance to the
Palace. M, court of the Megaron. B, North

26

against the rocky background of the north slope from the east end of the ramp (Figures 35* and 9).

The inner portico of the propylon (Fig. 35 No. 1) opens into a small court from which the west main passage begins (Fig. 35 No. 3). Most of the width of the passage at its north end was removed in the early excavations and so it is now but a narrow path; but originally it averaged a width of 6 meters. At the northeast corner of the passage the latest excavations revealed a stairway to a corridor (Fig. 35 Σ), mostly destroyed, that led to the apartments on the summit of the hill. The west main passage in a rising but gentle grade continues to the south and terminates in front of the great entrance to the palace proper, known as the western portal (Fig. 35 No. 4). Of that portal only its large conglomerate threshold, some 3.17 m. in length, survives. The structures which existed on its south side are completely gone, but on its north side we have a well preserved room that might have served as a guard room. In front and to the west of the portal was formed a tower-like court overlooking the western slope of the citadel. The view from that court is magnificent. In front of the citadel we see unfolding the rolling hills that formed the approach to the Lion Gate. In the foreground are the remains of Grave Circle B, the tholos tomb of Klytemestra, the houses revealed by Wace and Verdeles and believed to have been a perfume factory. Beyond the modern road rises the hill of Panayitsa with its small Chapel of Our Lady (Panayia); to it from the east leads a long stretch of rocky outcrop that looks like a Cyclopean wall, but which is the work of Nature. On that slope of the hill, the *dromos* or passage-way of the so-called Treasury of Atreus is clearly defined and beyond that stretches the plain of Argos limited to the west by crystalline mountains. The highest triangular peak is that of Mount Artemision, the sacred mountain of Arcadia. To the north of this is the Tretos mountain around the foothills of which the ancient and the modern road to Corinth and Athens winds its way. To the south, a conical hill indicates the location of Argos beyond which we have Mount Parthenion that stretches to the

27

direction of Tegea and Sparta. Indeed, the view from this court is magnificent.

The palace in its final form was constructed on the summit and on terraces on the southwest and east slopes of the hill; and so it had a multi-level appearance with one terrace rising above the other towards the summit. The best preserved and intelligible remains are on the southwest slope, which was artificially terraced. The main entrance to all the sections of the palace was through the west portal (Fig. 35 No. 4). From it started the south corridor (Fig. 35 No 6) an inclined ramp that, rising gradually, led to the apartments above the lower terrace. To the southwest of the west portal another narrower corridor (Fig. 35 No. 8) led to the southwest terrace where are to be found the best preserved sections of the palace. And as luck would have it these sections were among the most important and significant; they were the public sections of the palace where rooms for guests were to be found and where the king received audiences, entertained guests and friends and held his banquets.

THE GREAT COURT AND THE MEGARON
(Figure 35 Nos. 9 and 10).

Corridor No. 8 leads to a large court some 11 meters by 15 meters, open to the sky. Its floor originally was covered with plaster that was divided into squares and painted. On its east side stood the megaron, the most important unit of the palace (Fig. 35 No. 10); a long and narrow roofed structure with one of its short sides — the west side — opening to the court in the form of a portico with two columns between projecting side walls. The columns were made of wood and were destroyed in the great conflagration that ruined the palace, but the bases were of stone, and these survive. The floor of the portico (called in Homeric poetry the *aithousa*) was paved with slabs of gypsum stone imported from Crete. A few fragments are still in position on its south section and they indicate that there once were two shallow

Fig. 9. Preserved Steps of North Staircase

basins in the floor for libations to be poured by guests and host. The portico measures 3.85 m. in depth and 11.65 m. in width. A threshold in the north side of the portico indicates that there was a wooden stairway leading to the second terrace to apartments, perhaps to the women's quarter of the palace. The walls of the portico were covered with plaster and decorated with frescoes not preserved. The appearance of these walls is interesting and shows how the fire that destroyed the building transformed its rubble walls into a calcined mass of concrete hardness. This resulted from the use of timber chasing in the wall construction, which was usual to the Mycenaeans.

A well preserved conglomerate threshold leads to the vestibule, or the *prodomos* of the suite. On the south side of the threshold as we enter, a pivot hole is partially preserved and in this Tsountas found fragments of bronze with which was shod the

29

end of the pole around which the door revolved. The *prodomos* is deeper than the *aithousa* measuring 4.30 m. in depth. With the exception of its south wall its sides stand to a considerable height and in many parts have preserved coarse plaster over which was laid the final coat with fresco decoration. As a matter of fact fragments of frescoes were found in this vestibule and are now in the National Museum of Athens. The south wall of the vestibule, as well as the south side of the megaron, had collapsed into the Chavos ravine that flanks the south slope of the hill, and only recently has been restored to make the ground plan of the megaron intelligible. Around the walls of the vestibule there is a border 1 to 1.15 m. wide made of gypsum slabs; the central area of the floor within this border was covered with plaster and gaily painted. A small fragment of the painted floor is preserved below the pile of earth on the north section of the vestibule.

A large door opening led from the *prodomos,* or vestibule, to the main room of the megaron, the *domos.* Its threshold, still in position, suffered from the destructive fire of the catastrophe. This opening was not closed by a door but perhaps by a curtain when necessary. The same arrangement has been noticed in the Mycenaean palaces of Tiryns and of Pylos. The *domos,* or main room, is an imposing unit. At its preserved north side it measures 12.95 meters in depth; its width, as restored, amounts to 11.50 meters. The entire south side of the room, most of its east side, and a little over one third of its floor adjacent to the south and east walls had caved into the Chavos and were recently restored. In the middle of the floor stood a round hearth some 3.40 m. in diameter, one third of which survives. (It is now outlined with a single row of stones and covered with earth for preservation). It was built with a ring of poros stone enclosing a center of clay; both were covered with plaster that was renewed and painted from time to time (some ten layers of painted plaster were distinguished in the part that survived). The hearth rose only 0.15 m. above the floor of the room and constituted its central feature. It was surrounded by four wooden columns, the bases of three of

30

which are in their original position; the fourth, at the south east section, was restored (Figure 35 No. 10).

The central part of the floor was of stucco and this, divided by painted double lines into squares, was surrounded by a border of gypsum slabs running along the wall. The north and west walls at the northwest corner are preserved to a considerable height and originally were covered with frescoes fragments of which were found and are now in the National Museum at Athens. In these fragments are to be seen warriors with horses and chariots as well as women standing on a rocky ground. Another section seems to represent a battle scene. In the *domos* was the throne of the king; at the central part of the south wall, to the right of a person entering. Unfortunately that part of the *domos* is not preserved but the location of the throne can be established by analogy to the palaces of Tiryns and Pylos. Seated on his throne the king would receive his distinguished guests, or the ambassadors of other states. He could look across the hearth and see the frescoes depicting battle scenes, perhaps military successes of his ancestors or even of his own.

In the domos banquets were given similar to those described in the *Odyssey* as occuring in the Palace of Alkinoös in Phaeacia and in the Palace of Menelaos at Sparta. And perhaps the chairs or thrones of the banqueters, were placed on the border of gypsum slabs so as not to damage the stuccoed floor.

Above the ruins of the *domos,* northward rises Mount Prophet Elias, so-called because of the small chapel standing at its peak. On that peak were found the remnants of a Mycenaean look-out post and from that peak fire signals were flashed, indicating the occurrence of important events. By such a fire was signaled the fall of Troy; Aeschylos in his *Agamemnon* relates the story of the sentinel placed by Klytemestra on the roof of the megaron to watch the mountain peak and warn her when the fires would signal the arrival of Agamemnon. Tales turn into history and into reality for those who, standing in the megaron of the Palace of

Agamemnon, see the landmarks mentioned in the legends so vividly projecting against a blue sky. And when black, rainclouds sit heavily on the brows of Mt. Elias and Zara and ominously hover over citadel and plain the same landmarks and rugged mountains become the vivid reminders of the violent deeds that piled misfortune on the House of Atreus and on Mycenae.

From the portico of the megaron across the court to the west there is an almost square room, measuring 5.50 m. from north to south and 6.20 m. from east to west, fronted by a small court open to the sky (Fig. 35 No. 11). Against the north wall of the room a hearth was found by Tsountas and fragments of painted stucco found along its walls indicate that these were covered with frescoes. The room has wrongly been identified as a throne room. All parallels indicate that the throne of the king was in the *domos* of the megaron and the area here taken to be the place where stood a throne actually was a fire place. The square room and perhaps a smaller one which might have served as a bathroom, next to it to the west, not preserved, constituted an apartment for housing the guests of the royal family. The square room was a guest room located in the proximity of the megaron and away from the family section of the palace.

To the court in front of the guest room led the Grand Stairway that was built at the southwest corner of the palace (Fig. 35 No. 12). Of that stairway to be seen below the southside of the court, the first flight of 22 steps survives, low and wide of tread, with risers 0.10 - 0.12 m. in height. Where the steps terminate there was a landing platform, not preserved now, from which the second flight of steps began at right angles to the first to reach a second landing level with the court of the guest room. In front of the stairway, we find the «West Lobby» against the north and west walls of which run a low bench of stone and clay, originally covered with stucco. Here visitors might sit and rest before ascending the stairway, guards could wait and check the visitors, or members of the royal household could rest.

32

Before leaving the court the visitor should again look at the view of the Argive plain that like a picture spreads below the citadel. It does contrast with the rugged appearance of Mount Zara that raises its forbidding rocky mass along the south side of the citadel from which it is separated by the awe inspiring Chavos ravine. Today the rocky slopes are animated by herds of goats that nimbly roam' over impossible paths, adding to the varied spectacle. It may have been so in the days of old.

The upper terrace of the palace is now reached through the south corridor that begins at the west portal (Fig. 35 No. 6). It is 2.70 m. wide and originally it was paved with what is usually called Mycenaean lime-cement. Fragments of this pavement are preserved alongside the walls. Originally the south corridor led to a series of rooms to which later access was obtained through the wooden stairway located beyond the north end of the *aithousa* (or portico) of the megaron. Of these rooms most interesting is a rather long and narrow compartment (Fig. 35 No. 7), some 6 m. by 3.50 m., in which stone benches, a hearth, and fragments of painted plaster were found. These fragments from its walls were covered with painted designs of a unique subject; instead of figured compositions we find on them represented hangings of tapestries or curtains. Because of these frescoes I call the compartment the «Gallery of the Curtain Frescoes».

To the east of the gallery a stairway, now restored, led up to the domestic quarters of the palace. Of these quarters now scanty remains survive, and of these only one room has received especial attention (Fig. 35 No. 14). Its preserved northwest corner indicates that the room had a floor painted red and at least two steps or low benches along its sides. A drain at its north side and the color of its floor suggested to the native imagination the probability that this was the «red bath» in which Agamemnon was murdered! The evidence is against this interpretation but popular fancy persists.

Where the course of the south corridor is now interrupted by a crosswall and along its north side perhaps existed a staircase that led to a broad and long terrace running from east to west, then to the north corridor above it and the compartments on the summit of the hill. Of these scanty traces remain, and cannot be easily detected. The uppermost terrace of the palace was used over and over again in the course of the centuries of the Historic Era. A large temple dedicated to Athena or Hera was constructed on it in the third century B.C. That temple was oriented north and south and the foundations of its walls are the only conspicuous and intelligible architectural remains on the summit. (Fig. 35, the foundations are indicated by stones in outline.) To these foundations belong the large blocks of poros stone and conglomerate, even two bases of a Mycenaean column, that form the large rectangular base of the temple.

The palace extended beyond the summit to the east slope which was artificially terraced in three levels. The topmost of these begins as the lonely almond tree that forms the only conspicuous landmark of the summit (Fig. 35 No. 16). Here begins the path to the east section of the citadel. Of the rooms that might have existed on the first and second levels or terraces only a few stones remain scattered here and there but sufficient to prove that the palace extended in this direction. On the second terrace the foundations of a long portico built of reused Mycenaean blocks but belonging to the third century B.C. are noticeable. The second terrace at its southeast side terminated in a broad corridor below which, to the east, rose the structure on the third terrace.

ARTISTS QUARTERS (Figure 36 Z).

One may descend to that terrace by means of a modern stairway constructed for the convenience of the visitors. The rooms cut in the rock to the south of the stairway (to the right as we descend) that are noticeable from it belong to the third century B.C. On the third terrace just beyond the visitors' stairway to the south, were lately uncovered remains of a large Mycenaean building over the remains of which another building was con-

34

structed in the third century B.C. The ground plan of the later building cannot be determined now; its foundations lying close to the surface were mostly destroyed in the course of time. But the plan of the Mycenaean building can be made out clearly (Fig. 36 Z). It is composed of a long and narrow court open to the sky (Fig. 36 Z No. 1) flanked by two narrow corridors the easternmost of which is clearly defined and easily noticed (Fig. 36 Z No. 2). From these corridors access was obtained into a series of rooms, four on the east side and, on a higher level, four on the west. The difference in levels and three preserved steps of a stairway prove that over the corridors and the four rooms on the east side rose a second story corresponding in plan to the ground level. The building, some 28 m. by 30 m. is substantial; its plan, position and the finds made in it prove that it formed part of the East Wing of the palace and served the artists and artisans of the royal family. It formed the artists quarters and workrooms.

«HOUSE OF COLUMNS» (Figure 36 E).

Immediately to the east and below the artists quarters stood what Wace called the «House of Columns». The foundations of this building can now be made out easily. The Cyclopean retaining wall, supporting the terrace on which were built the four east rooms of the artists quarters, forms the north limit of a long corridor leading from the doorway, indicated by its threshold still in position (Fig. 36 E No. 3), to a central court open to the sky (Fig. 36 E No. 4) and surrounded by columns. Some of the column bases are still in place; these columns gave the name to the building. Beyond the east side of the court stood a megaron and next to it a staircase (Fig. 36 E No. 4) leading to a second story over the south side of the building that is not preserved. Along the west side of the court there was a series of compartments, non-existant now, below which are still to be seen basement rooms and corridors (Fig. 36 E No. 5).

The building is known as the «House of Columns», but the

Fig. 10. Remains of Building A in the Northeast Extension. Upper left Corner: Pithos Room. Lower, Section of a Tub

excavations of 1967 and 1968 have proved that it formed part of the Palace, that it was its East Wing, perhaps occupied by a member of the royal family. It was constructed in the second half of the 13th century and was destroyed by fire about 1200 B.C. Partially rebuilt after that fire, it was finally destroyed about 1120 B.C.

To the right and left of the modern path, leading to the east end of the citadel, were revealed the foundations of two buildings, Δ and Γ, with a number of basement rooms for the storage of the possessions of the kings. These buildings are now proved to have belonged to the palace complex which extended from the summit eastward to the double dotted line of Figure 36. Thus the palace of Mycenae is proved to have been the most extensive palace on the mainland of Greece.

THE NORTHEAST EXTENSION (Figure 36 A, B, H).

The northeast end of the citadel is a rather narrow area surrounded by heavy fortification walls. It is the latest addition to the fortified area and is known as the northeast extension. Until recently it was maintained that it was added to the citadel to provide an open space where people and the horses of the king could take refuge in times of hostile invasions. The excavations of 1963, however, proved that the greater part of its area was taken by two buildings, Alpha and Beta. The extension was made to remedy one of the great weaknesses of the citadel, the lack of an adequate water supply. There is not a spring on the hill, and the few wells existing on it and the cisterns constructed for the storage of rain water were not sufficient to insure the water supply of a beleagered population. This was achieved by the construction of a subterranean cistern to which water was brought by means of an underground aqueduct from hidden springs in the slopes of Prophet Elias, some distance from the citadel. (The visitor should be equipped with a torch if he intends to visit the lower sections of the cistern.)

THE UNDERGROUND CISTERN (Figures 11 Y and 36 Y).

The opening to the cistern is at the northeast corner of the extension and in the north Cyclopean wall. It is in the form of a corbel arch of the interted V type so characteristic of late Mycenaean construction. It is protected from the slope above it by a retaining wall which in the third century B.C. was projected further to the south to almost block half of the width of the extension. The subterranean cistern is the most striking surviving construction on the citadel and is composed of three parts. The first section is a descending stepped passage formed obliquely through the north Cyclopean wall with its arched (corbelled) opening approached from the interior of the citadel. Sixteen of the original steps are still preserved and they terminate in a

37

Fig. 11. Entrance to Underground Cistern, Y. North Sally Port, H

small rectangular platform that is underground and outside the wall. The second section, beginning at the southwest side of the platform, has 20 preserved steps leading westward to a landing some 2.30 m. below the level of the first. Three steps on the north side of the landing take us to the third stage of the passage that now turns at right angles and proceeds steeply downwards towards the northeast. Some 54 steps below, and about 12 m. deeper, the passage terminates at a well-like cistern about 1.60 m. by 0.70 m. and 5 m. deep. Immediately above the cistern in the roof of the passage there is a large opening at which terminated the water conduit of terracotta pipes, the aqueduct. The steps and the walls of the third section are covered with a thick coat of water-tight plaster; evidently part of the stepped passage acted also as a cistern. The passage as well as the entire subterranean cistern is an awe-inspiring Cyclopean construction. Some scholars believe that this underground cistern is the Perseia Fountain mentioned by Pausanias, but it is doubtful that he went as far as the northeast extension of the citadel and most probably the fountain mentioned by him was located outside the walls.

«THE NORTH SALLY PORT» (Figures 11 H and 36 H).

Next to this underground cistern there is an opening through the north Cyclopean wall; it is a sally port from which the defenders could suddenly rush and surprise an enemy attacking the Postern Gate. Immediately to the northeast of the «North Sally Port» is a round open cistern belonging to the third century B.C., when the subterranean cistern was no longer in use.

In 1963 and in the northeast section of the extension we revealed structure Beta (Fig. 36 B) with a number of rooms. Its

Fig. 12.
South Sally Port

location so near the subterranean cistern makes it possible to assume that it was occupied by an official who was entrusted with the supervision and security of this most important establishment; so we call it «the Water Commissioner's House».

«THE SOUTH SALLY PORT» (Figure 12).

Across from structure Beta and in the south Cyclopean wall there is another passage known as the «South Sally Port». It pierces the Cyclopean wall in a straight line and has a length of some 7.10 meters and a height of 2.50 m. Its roof is in the form of a corbel vault of the inverted V type. It led to a natural platform adjacent to the south Cyclopean wall that served as a look-out post over the Chavos ravine. The view to the west from this platform is really striking. (To the east beyond the poplar trees on the nearby hills is to be found the Perseia spring that still supplies water to Mycenae.)

The south half of the extension was occupied by another building (Alpha) of which only a basement room survives. At the time of the excavation (1963) it contained among other things the fragments of six large storage jars or *pithoi*. Outside of the basement the greater part of a terracotta bath tub was found in position (Fig. 11). Between buildings Alpha and Beta there was a lane some 1.70 m. wide. Just beyond the point where the south wall of building Beta terminates in an *anta*, the lane turned to the right and proceeded to the north Cyclopean wall. Its continuation was found below the modern path that was created alongside the retaining wall which protects the opening of the subterranean cistern. (The visitor will do well to take this path on his way back to the Lion Gate thus avoiding a climb to the summit of the hill.)

On reaching the north Cyclopean wall the lane turned again at right angles and proceeded westward between the wall and building *Gamma*. At the corner of *Gamma* it forked to the south, while its main section continued towards the Postern Gate. The branch to the south ascends the hill to reach a court from which

40

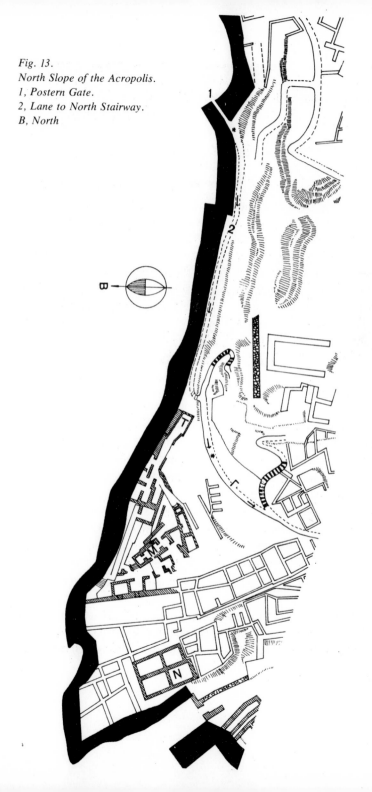

Fig. 13.
North Slope of the Acropolis.
1, Postern Gate.
2, Lane to North Stairway.
B, North

Fig. 14. North (N) and South (S) Retaining Wall of Main Road (Γ)

access was obtained to buildings *Gamma* and *Delta*, to the *House of Columns*, the *Artists Quarters* and the east section of the palace. The main section of the lane continued westward to terminate at a stairway, partially preserved, that descends to the inner court of the Postern Gate.

Above this continuation a series of store rooms was revealed in 1969. In these rooms can be seen the restored storage jars which were found in fragments.

THE POSTERN GATE (Figure 13 No. 1).

The gate was built on the same principles and with the same material as the Lion Gate, after the middle of the 13th century B.C. Four large blocks of conglomerate worked to shape by hammer and saw form a door opening 2.30 meters high and 1.40 m. wide at the threshold. The opening narrows slightly upwards. Two pivot holes in the lintel indicate that the opening was closed by a double wooden door, similar to the one restored. When shut, the door was secured fast by a wooden beam that slid into sockets cut in the doorposts. Instead of a relieving triangle over the lintel, two slabs were placed so as to leave an empty space between them. The slabs are supported at their two ends and thus their weight is conveyed to the posts. In front of the gate a narrow corridor is formed, some 2.30 meters in width, between the north Cyclopean wall, on the south, and a bastion, on the north, recalling the court in front of the Lion Gate. At the inner side of the gate a small court was formed, some 4 m. by 4 m., at the south side of which a small room was made under the stairway of the lane from the northeast extension. This room was perhaps for guards or for watchdogs.

THE NORTH SLOPE OF THE CITADEL (Figure 13).

From the inner court a lane leads westward between the north Cyclopean wall and the abrupt north slope of the hill (Fig. 13 No. 2). That slope was retained by a heavy wall, remnants of which are still visible. The lane is crossed by walls of the third century B.C., but originally it went without interruption (Fig. 13 arrows) to the foot of the north stairway of the palace, now destroyed. In that area it met with the main road that came from the Lion Gate, two stretches of which still survive (Fig. 13 Γ). The retaining walls of the Main Road are well preserved (Fig. 14) and the visitor today actually walks on its westernmost section, reached by a few steps built a few years ago for the convenience of the visitors.

The main Mycenaean road Γ leads to the modern path that forms the northeastern branch of the ascending avenue from the Ramp to the Palace. To the north of the path in the years 1961 - 1964 we uncovered the foundations of a complex «Building M», with corridors and an adjacent stairway (Fig. 13 M). It is located above a series of corridors along the north Cyclopean wall leading into storerooms constructed within the thickness of that wall (Fig. 15). These storerooms were not part of the initial wall construction, but apparently were a later addition made perhaps in imitation of the galleries of Tiryns. Unfortunately only traces of these rooms are evident today because the upper sections of the north Cyclopean wall were destroyed in the course of the centuries and with them the rooms they enclosed. But it is proved that the walls, the corridors, and the rooms were kept in good

Fig. 15. Corridors and Stairway along the North Cyclopean Wall (BKT)

repair until the final destruction of the citadel at the end of the 12th century. The relation of «Building M» to the walls and storerooms and its peculiarities, each of its entrances seems to have been protected by a guardroom, lead us to maintain that its occupant was responsible for the defense of the walls, that he was in charge of the armaments and provisions kept in the storerooms for times of siege. We call therefore «Building M» «the Military Commander's Quarters».

To the west of «Building M», towards the Lion Gate, are evident a number of foundations. They were unearthed in the early days of the excavations at Mycenae and remain unrecorded. Their function, purpose, and even date remain uncertain. Some belong to the Mycenaean Age, others to the third century B.C. The structure immediately above the Lion Gate with walls in Cyclopean style (Fig. 13 N-hatched walls) belongs to the early part of the 12th century B.C. It is one of the latest buildings constructed in the citadel, and perhaps served to house its garrison.

The description of the remains in the citadel will indicate its function. It served as the area in which were built the palace of the king, the houses of the princely families and of the dignitaries of the state, buildings in which the warriors defending it could be housed, structures in which the provisions and treasures of the king and the state could be stored. In times of war and enemy invasions the citizens of the state found refuge in it. In the case of Mycenae, the graves of its ancient royal family were included within the citadel in the 13th century B.C. They formed a historic landmark, a kind of a heroön, respected and cared for because of its value to the living as a memorial reminding them and their visitors and friends of the grandeur and achievement of their ancestors. At the same time were constructed the Cult Center of Mycenae, with its shrines and altars, and the dwellings of its High Priest and personnel.

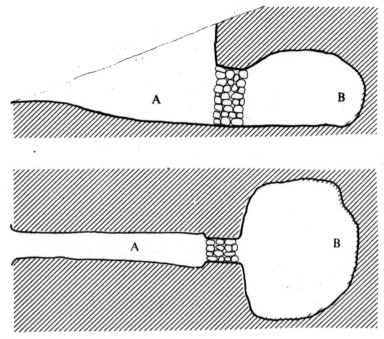

Fig. 16. Plan and Section of a Chamber Tomb
A, dromos, B, chamber

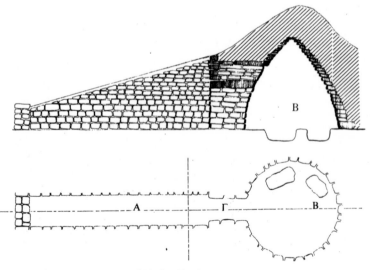

Fig. 17. Plan and Section of Tholos Tomb
A, dromos. B, chamber. Γ, stomion

PART II

REMAINS OUTSIDE THE CITADEL

To the west and northwest of the Citadel spreads the area where the citizenry lived. Traces of fortifications enclosing it do not belong to the Mycenaean Period but to the third century B.C. The citizenry of Mycenae in the Late Bronze Age lived in small detached family groups at a short distance from each other, with the graves of their ancestors surrounding their dwellings and with roads and lanes connecting their small subdivisions with each other and with the Citadel. And so we find remains of houses and graves outside the Citadel scattered over the adjacent hills. Before we visit them it will be helpful to have a description of the graves typical of the Late Bronze Age at Mycenae.

TYPES OF GRAVES

We have already seen that towards the end of the 17th and the beginning of the 16th century B.C. the shaft graves were used for the burial of royalty, that they seem to have been enclosed in a Grave Circle. The common people were buried in box-like graves made of slabs set vertically in the ground, and known as cist graves, or small trenches cut in the rock, a type that was ancestral. It seems that under influence from beyond the mainland of Greece, perhaps from Egypt, the Mycenaeans developed an underground, rock-cut family grave known as **Chamber Tomb** (Fig. 16). It is cut horizontally into the slope of a hillside and is composed of two parts: a long passage, known as *dromos,* that is

47

open to the sky, and a chamber hollowed out in the hillside like a cave. The chambers thus are underground and have a variety of shapes — round, oval, elliptical, rectangular etc. — depending on the hardness of the rock in which they are cut. Well-built door openings connected the passageways and the chambers, and these openings were blocked by a wall of stones after the burial. Within these underground chambers were laid the dead of a family for generations. Chamber tombs can be seen in the hills of Mycenae, even at the northeast side of the road (the righthand side as we descend from the citadel to the village). Some have imposing dimensions. For example, one of the largest (No. 505) has a *dromos* 35 meters long and a chamber 5.50 m. by 6.50 m. with a height of 6.50 to 7 meters.

Graves for the burial of royalty were more elaborate, although their parts were similar to those of the chamber tombs. They are known as the **Tholos** or **Beehive Tombs** (Fig. 17). They are built in the slopes of hills and are underground. They are approached by a passage, the *dromos*, open to the sky, and have an elaborate doorway and entranceway known as *stomion*, beyond which is to be found a round chamber, the burial chamber. This is roofed over by a stone corbel vault made up of horizontal rings of stone diminishing in diameter as they go upward. Because the chamber is round it was called by the Greeks *tholos*, from which is derived the name for the type used by scholars today. Again, because the corbel vaulting of its chamber in section looks like an old-fashioned beehive, these royal sepulchers are also called beehive tombs. Sometimes rectangular cists were cut in the floor of the chamber for the accommodation of the bodies and their most valuable gifts (example: the Lion Tomb).

At Mycenae nine tholos tombs are known to date. They present different structural characteristics illustrating the development of the type from a more primitive to a most developed stage. Wace, who was the first to make a scientific study of the graves, divides them into three distinct groups dating from different times from about 1550 to the end of the 13th century B.C. All the tholos tombs of Mycenae were emptied of their contents in the past. But a good many of the chamber tombs were found intact and their contents help us to determine the burial customs of the people. The chamber and tholos tombs remained the characteristic sepulchers of the Mycenaeans to the end of the age and are to be found in the entire Greek world of the Late Bronze Age.

THE LION THOLOS TOMB (Figure 32 No. 10).

Across the court and road from the Lion Gate to the guard house (on the right-hand side beyond the northwest corner of the fortification walls) and outside the wire fence, there is a very instructive tholos tomb. (The guard can be asked to open the small gate to the tomb.) It is known as the Lion Tomb, because it is so near the Lion Gate. It belongs to Wace's second group and apparently was constructed about the middle of the 14th century B.C. The top part of its vault has caved in and its debris cleared away and so the method of its construction is clear. Its *dromos,* or passageway, is 5.40 m. wide and 22 m. long. Its chamber has a diameter of 14 meters and the height of the vault is calculated to have been 15 meters. The façade of its doorway, built in conglomerate is covered by a veneer of ashlar work in poros stone and within its chamber are cut three pit graves found empty.

THE MIDDLE BRONZE AGE CEMETERY

The modern road from the Lion Gate to the exit turns sharply to the west. Near the turn on the south side (left as one goes out) of the road are the foundations of poros stone of a third century B.C. fountain which perhaps is the Perseia Fountain mentioned by Paysanias. Above its southwest corner begins a path leading in a southwesterly direction. Between this path and the west Cyclopean wall of the citadel existed a cemetery of the Early and the

Fig. 18. The so-called Tomb of Klytemestra

Pre-Mycenaean or Middle Bronze Age period made up of a number of cist graves and shafts cut in the rock. To the same cemetery belonged Grave Circle A, which, as we have seen above, originally was outside the citadel and only about 1250 B.C. was included in the fortified area.

THE «TOMB OF AIGISTHOS» (Figure 32 No. 11).

Somewhat beyond the cemetery to the left of the path we look down into the Tholos Tomb now known as that of Aigisthos. The top of the *tholos* has collapsed and is not preserved, but we can

50

again see the way its vault was constructed. A comparison of its vault to that of the Lion Tomb will indicate that the latter is of a later and more advanced construction. The so-called Tomb of Aigisthos belongs to the first and earliest group of beehive tombs as distinguished by Wace. Its round chamber has a diameter of over 13 meters, and its *dromos* or passageway cut in the soft rock, a width of 4 to 5 m. and a length of 22 meters.

THE «TOMB OF KLYTEMESTRA»
(Figures 18 and 32 No. 12).

The path descending the slope will take us to the beginning of the *dromos* of the so-called tomb of Klytemestra. This is the latest of the tholos tombs built at Mycenae and it seems to have been constructed around 1220 B.C. The rock-cut passageway or *dromos* measures 37 meters in length and 6 m. in width, and its sides are lined with more or less rectangular conglomerate blocks

Fig. 19. Grave Circle B. Contents of Grave Upsilon (Y)

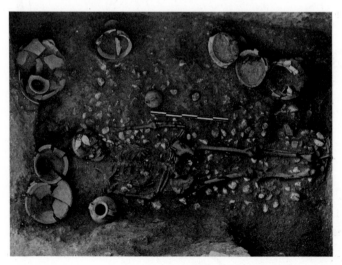

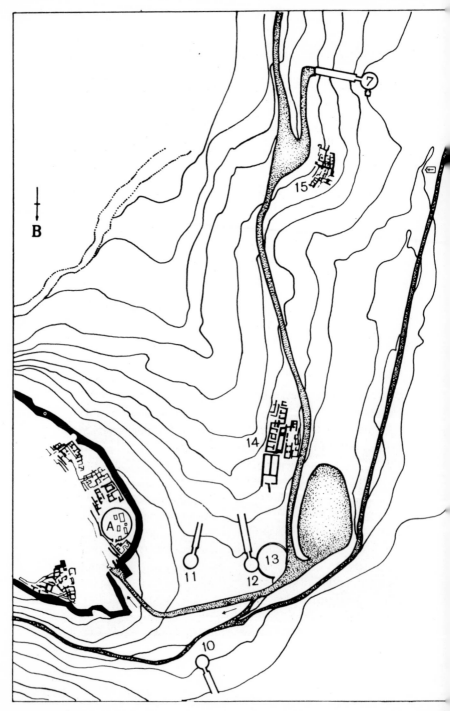

Fig. 20. Plan of the Area outside the Walls. B, North

placed in horizontal courses (Fig. 18). The façade of its entranceway was once covered with marble incrustation. On either side of the door opening are in their original position bases on which stood attached half-columns of gypsum with thirteen flutings. The relieving triangle over the lintel, and, as a matter of fact, the entire entablature was masked by marble slabs covered with elaborate carvings, spirals, rosettes, etc., placed in horizontal bands. The deep entranceway, or *stomion,* was closed by a door of wood placed about the middle of its length. The round chamber has a diameter of 13.50 meters with a corbel vault of 13 m. in height, as restored. (The original vaulting is preserved to a height of 8.55 m.) Noticeable in the vaulting is the wider band that continues the height of the lintel around the vault, relieving the uniformity of the courses and providing a firm base for the corbel vault. The Tomb of Klytemestra, as restored, is one of the impressive monuments of the Mycenaean world and one of the latest examples of tholos tombs at Mycenae.

This tholos tomb was detected between the years 1807 and 1812; the exact date remains uncertain. In building their aqueduct the villagers accidentally placed its channel over the top of the tomb and thus discovered its apex. Veli the Pasha of Nafplion, who was at the time the Turkish governor of the district, destroyed the top of the vault and through that opening removed the contents of the tholos. No description of what was found is preserved, although the imagination of the people has conjured up loads of gold and silver carried away by teams of mules. The tomb was unknown even to the inhabitants of the third century B.C., for across its *dromos* they built their theater. One row of seats of that theater can still be seen on either side of the *dromos* and by the steep path that leads to the north from the entrance of the passageway. That passageway was investigated by Madame Schliemann and by Tsountas who found about the middle of its length an undisturbed burial containing valuable gifts.

Neither this nor the partially preserved tholos tomb above it is the Tomb of Klytemestra or the Tomb of Aigisthos. The names

Fig. 21. Grave Circle B. Contents of Grave Gamma (Γ)

were given to the sepulchers by the villagers at the time of their clearing and have no relation to reality. They were adopted by scholars as identifying labels with the specific understanding that they were not the graves of the persons whose names they now bear. We do not know who were the people buried in them, but since the Tomb of Klytemestra is the latest in date of the tholos tombs known, it may belong to Agamemnon and his descendants.

Fig. 22. Plan of Grave Circle B (Drawing by D. Theochares)

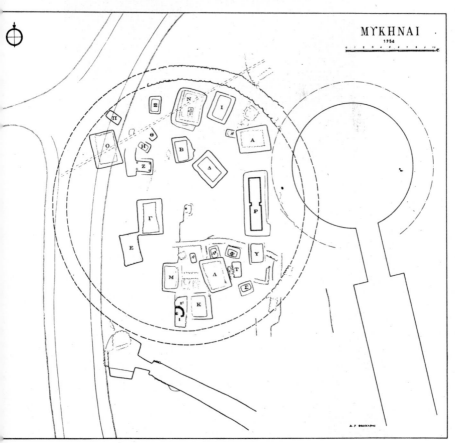

Fig. 23. Grave Circle B. Rock Crystal Duck - Bowl from Grave Omicron (O)

GRAVE CIRCLE B
(Figures 20 No. 13, 19, 21, 22, 25 and 32 No. 13).

The ascending path from the Tomb of Klytemestra leads to Grave Circle B. The area enclosed in this circle has an estimated diameter of about 28 meters (Fig. 25 Restoration). The parapet wall enclosing it is preserved for a length of some 18 meters on the north side, towards the modern road, and it was built of large stones rising to a height of one meter. The Circle was excavated in the summer of 1952, 1953, 1954 and 1955 and the contents of its graves are exhibited in the National Archaeological Museum of Athens (objects of gold, silver, bronze, rock crystal and some vases) and in the Museum of Nafplion (vases and stelai). A total of 24 graves were found and explored in Circle B; they were given the letters of the Greek alphabet by which they are now identified. Of the graves fourteen are royal shaft graves, the rest are cist and trench tombs. Structurally they are similar to the shaft and cist graves found in Circle A and their dimensions are analogous. The largest shaft grave, Gamma, almost in the center of the circular area, measures at the top 3.80 m. in length and 2.80 m. in width; its depth is 3.50 m. The smallest, Grave Xi, the sepulcher of a small princess, measures 2.75 by 1.80 meters and is 2 meters deep. In three of the shaft graves only one skeleton was found, in the rest from two to four skeletons. Grave Gamma contained four skeletons (Fig. 21). Around the bodies, dressed in fineries and ornaments, were arranged gifts and possessions including many vases containing supplies to be used in the long trip to the lower world (Fig. 19). No traces of wooden coffins, of embalming, or of

Fig. 24. Grave Circle B. Grave Rho (P)

cremation were found and apparently the bodies were laid on a floor of pebbles over which occasionally a pelt was placed. Next to vases the most common objects found were swords and dagers of bronze, while gold bands decorated in repoussé, were discovered in burials of men as well as of women. Other objects include gold and silver cups, necklaces of gold beads, of semi-precious stones and beads of amber, rings of gold, silver, and bronze, earrings of gold and silver, bronze and silver pins with heads of rock crystal, one mask made of electrum, and a tiny bead of

Fig. 25. Restoration of Grave Circle B (Drawing by A. Voyatzis)

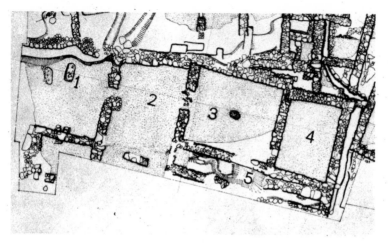

Fig. 26. Ground Plan of House I (Drawing by K. Schaar)

amethyst on which is engraved the head of a Mycenean leader in a powerful style. Grave Omikron, the grave of a royal princess, in addition yielded a wonderful rock crystal bowl in the form of a duck some 13.5 cm. in extreme length (Figure 23). Perhaps it was used by the princess for the mixing of perfumes and colors used for her personal adornment. Now it is in the National Museum of Athens.

The skeletal remains found indicate that the men buried in Circle B were sturdy individuals averaging 1.706 m. (5´7 1/8´´) in height and at least three of them were over 1.80 m. tall. Women were shorter averaging 1.50 m. (4´11´´) in height. One of the individuals buried in grave Gamma had suffered a skull fracture, to relieve which a trepanation was performed; one of the oldest skull operations on record in the history of medicine of the western world. Two gall stones were found among the bones of the individual buried in Grave Sigma and he as well as others suffered from arthritis as well.

Grave Rho of Circle B is now covered by a concrete roof and its entrance is barred. Originally it was a shaft grave. In the second half of the 15th century B.C. it was enlarged and within it was built of poros stone another grave possessing a passage and a burial chamber (Fig. 24). It is a unique (for Greece) and remarkable example of a built grave parallels to which exist in Ras Shamra, in Syria. Unfortunately, it was emptied of its contents in antiquity.

Chronologically Grave Circle B and its graves belong to the end of the 17th and the first half of the 16th century B.C. Some of its graves are contemporary to those of Grave Circle A, others are older. All of them, however, indicate that in those centuries Mycenae had already become wealthy and powerful since their ruling families could afford to deposit so many valuable objects in graves without fear of their security.

HOUSES OF MERCHANTS, OR PERFUME WORKSHOP
(Fig. 20 No. 14).

Within the area surrounded by the fence and some 75 meters to the south of Grave Circle B are to be seen the foundations of what were taken by their excavators to belong to four different buildings. The westernmost foundations, nearest to the modern road, excavated by N. Verdeles, belong to what he called the West House. The others, to the east belong to what Wace called the House of the Sphinxes, the House of the Oil Merchant, and the House of Shields. The first and third were so called from objects in ivory with representations of sphinxes or in the form of shields. The second, or middle structure was so called because in one of its basement rooms remnants of pithoi were found, in which oil evidently was stored and cared for in the winter months. In these buildings were found tablets in Linear B script, records of various accounts and lists of people. Herbs and aromatic plants are mentioned also and because of this and the installations of the pithoi many scholars believe that these were not houses of merchants but a royal factory for the manufacture of perfumed oil.

The group of buildings was destroyed by fire towards the end of the 13th century B.C. and its ruins were abandoned. (Perhaps it will prove sufficient to inspect these foundations from the modern road from which they are separated by a fence. For this the visitors will have to leave the fenced area by the door near the guard house where tickets are sold and follow the modern road back towards the direction of the village.)

At some 200 meters to the south of this group of buildings, outside the areas enclosed by the fence and on the west side of the modern road there is a small parking area lined with pines. This is at the east slope of the hill known as the Hill of Panayitsa because of the little white chapel that stands at its summit. Immediately behind the pines and the fence (to the west) foundations of a group of houses are being brought to light by the current excavations (Fig. 20 No. 15). They illustrate the type of houses used by

Fig. 27.
Broken Vessels
around Hearth
of House I.
Skeleton of Woman
on Threshold
of Doorway

Fig. 28. Treasury of Atreus

the Mycenaean citizens, perhaps of the middle-class. They have a central room corresponding to the megaron of the palace, with a round or rectangular hearth at the center, and a number of rooms, basements and corridors around them. They are usually entered from a court open to the sky.

The plan of the house at the southernmost end of the excavated area, of House I, can be easily made out even from behind the wire fence (Fig. 26). At the extreme left is the court open to the sky (No. 1). Following it (No. 2) is a comparatively shallow room, the forehall to the main room (No. 3) that at its center possesses a round hearth rising some 20 cm. above the paved floor. (Both floor and hearth are covered with earth for better preservation.) In the rear of the main room is a smaller compartment (No. 4), while along the east side of these rooms exists a corridor (No. 5) to the east of which are the east rooms of the house now under the fence. The house was destroyed by an earthquake about 1250 B.C. One of its inhabitants (the lady of the house or a slave?) was crushed by the collapsed walls and her skeleton was found on the threshold of the central room (Fig. 27). The foundations of these houses enable us to study the domestic architecture of the Mycenaens as the foundations in the citadel made possible the study of their palace architecture.

THE TREASURY OF ATREUS (Figures 28 and 29).

In the same hill of Panayitsa and somewhat to the south of its group of houses is one of the most impressive monuments of the Mycenaean Age, the tholos tomb known to the students and scholars as the Treasury of Atreus and to the villagers as the tomb of Agamemnon. It is completely preserved with only the decoration of its façade and interior missing. As the visitor stands at the north end of its passage and looks towards the façade he cannot help but wonder at the people who built such monuments to house their dead kings (Fig. 28).

The passageway, or *dromos,* cut in the rock of the hillside, is lined with rectangular conglomerate blocks some of which are very large in size (one block along the base course at the right-hand side measures 6 meters in length and 1.25 m. in height). The width of the *dromos* amounts to 6 meters, while its length is 36 m. The west end of the *dromos* is blocked by the façade of the grave that rises to a height of 10.50 meters. The monumental proportions of its doorway are evident (5.40 m. high and 2.70 m. wide at the threshold and 2.45 m. wide at the top).

Two receding fasciae are carved in the masonry and carried around to frame the doorway which is spanned by an enormous lintel. Above it we have the characteristic relieving triangle. On either side of the doorway a rectangular base can still be seen in its original position. The bases are made of three superposed plinths on which half-columns once stood secured to the façade by dowels. (Now only the dowel holes can be seen in the mason-

63

Fig. 29. Façade of Treasury of Atreus: Restoration of the Decoration (Drawing by Ch. Williams)

ry.) Fragments of the columns made of greenish stone and elaborately decorated in relief are now to be seen in the National Museum of Athens and in the British Museum. In the same museums are to be seen fragments of carved slabs that covered the façade above the lintel and closed the relieving triangle (Fig. 29).

The *stomion,* or entranceway, is deep and is roofed by two blocks or lintels. The innermost of the two, seen in the interior of the *tholos* as well, measures 9 meters in length by 5 m. in width and 1.20 m. in thickness; its estimated weight amounts to 120 tons. In spite of its weight, it is beautiful fitted in its position, and its face on the *tholos* is worked so as to carry the double curvature of the wall.

The main round room measures 14.60 meters in diameter on the ground and its corbel vault has a height of almost 13.50 m. It is made up of 33 superposed courses (or rings) of perfectly joined conglomerate blocks. On the face of its walls, from the third course upward, we find holes and remnants of bronze nails that secured once bronze decorations on the walls such as rosettes and spirals. Its floor, cut in the solid rock, originally was covered with hard-packed whitish earth. On that floor the bodies to be buried were laid.

On the north side of the *tholos* there is a doorway surmounted by a lintel and a relieving triangle leading through a passageway to a side chamber about 5.80 m. high and 6 m. square, cut in the soft conglomerate of the hill. This is an unusual feature in tholos tomb construction, with only one other example known in the «Treasury of Minyas» at Orchomenos.

A mere glance at the tholos will prove sufficient to conclude that it is the greatest known engineering achievement of the Mycenaean Age. The planning and skill in construction, its proportions and lofty vault, the care with which the rings of stone were fitted and smoothed, the apparent facility with which the huge blocks were carved to fit a round structure and were eased in their positions, indicate the high degree of excellence attained

65

by the architects of the 13th century B.C. The grave was probably emptied in antiquity perhaps and nothing survives of its original furnishings. We wish it were possible to visualize the burial ritual held in this magnificent sepulcher, to recover its interior as it was left when the body of the last king was deposited on its floor and a solid wall of stones was built across its entranceway! But the contents of the grave were gone long before the days of Pausanias and all we have left is the varied pictures our imagination can provide as it is stimulated by the massive architectural remains.

There can be no doubt that this tholos tomb is the one called by Pausanias the Treasury of Atreus, that it was so known to people who lived at Mycenae at the time of the traveler's visit. Possibly by this name it was known in Classical times, when graves of this type were no longer produced and when their actual function had been forgotten. Again we may maintain that tradition had preserved the association of monument and king who constructed it, that consequently this tholos was constructed by Atreus and served as his grave. Perhaps its contents were found and dispersed at a time in antiquity when tholos tombs had been forgotten, perhaps so many objects of gold and other valuable metals were found in it that the people who plundered it assumed it was the treasury of the king whose name was associated with the monument, and so they called it the Treasury of Atreus. The skeletons found in it may have been assumed as belonging to robbers who could not find the exit after they had entered bent on robbing it. One recalls the story of a similar monument of Pharaoh Rameses III recorded by Herodotos. An explanation of the name could thus be suggested and the possible conclusion that this tholos tomb is the sepulcher of Atreus could be confidently projected. Of course, it cannot be maintained that it is the grave of Agamemnon as the villagers want, since that king lived at a somewhat later date.

This brings us to the date of the monument. It was maintained for a long time that this tholos tomb was built around 1330 B.C.,

Fig. 30. Terracotta statuette from the Mycenaean Shrine of the thirteenth century B.C.

that it was built at the same time as the Lion Gate. The latest excavations proved that the Lion Gate was built around 1250 B.C. and around the middle of the 13th century B.C. the tholos was constructed. We may now note that the traditional date of the reign of Atreus agrees with this date since he is recorded as ruling Mycenae around the middle of the 13th century B.C.

On the way to the village from the Treasury of Atreus on the side of the road to the right are apparent the passageways, or *dromoi,* of chamber tombs that look like dark caverns. Before reaching the village on the left-hand side of the road the remnants of a viaduct spanning the ravine are visible. It seems to have been constructed at the very end of the 13th century B.C., if not at the beginning of the 12th, and it marks the end of a road that connected Mycenae with Argos.

NOTE: If time permits it may prove interesting to visit another intact tholos tomb known to the villagers as the «Tomb of Orestes», but certainly not the sepulcher of that king. It is somewhat older than the «Treasury of Atreus» and much smaller, but it is completely preserved. The scholars call it the «Tomb of the Genii» from a few small plaques of glass paste bearing a decoration of genii found in its chamber. This tholos tomb was also emptied of its contents in the past. To find it will require the services of a villager. On the way and in the adjacent hills the visitor will see a good number of chamber tombs and three tholos tombs, whose remains are very scanty and not so interesting.

A kilometer and a half to the North of the citadel the latest excavations revealed a sanctuary dedicated to the war God Ares. The sanctuary belongs to the third century B.C. and is composed of a temple, its altars, and an auxiliary building for the storing of offerings. Among these were found the fragments of a shield which, as the inscription punched on it states, was dedicated by the Argives from the spoils taken from Pyrrhus king of Epeiros who was killed at Argos ca. 272 B.C. A guide will be required for the visit of this sanctuary.

PART III

LEGENDS AND HISTORY

The study of its ruins makes it evident that Mycenae was one of the most important cultural and political centers of Greece in the Heroic Age. Some scholars maintain that it was the capital city of a great Empire, known to the Hittites as *Ahhiyawâ*.

By nature Mycenae was destined to play a leading role in the affairs of Greece. Situated in the northeastern corner of the plain of Argos, «in the nook of horse-pasturing Argos», between two mountains, Mount Prophet Elias to the north (height 2645 feet) and Zara to the south (2170 feet), Mycenae dominated the plain and controlled the overland routes to the north, the west, the east, and even the sea lane of the gulf of Nafplion through its dependency, the citadel of Tiryns. That is, it controlled the commercial routes of southeastern Greece and to that could be attributed its prosperity and cultural activity. The importance of its location was recognized at an early age and so Greek legends tell us that Mycenae was founded by Perseus, son of Zeus and Danaë and destroyer of the Gorgon Medusa; it was he, they state, who fortified its citadel using the Cyclopes for the construction of its walls. He sired the Perseid dynasty that ruled over Mycenae and its territories for at least three generations. Eurystheus, one of his descendants, was the king for whom the Tirynthian Heracles performed his storied exploits, and perhaps these tales indicate the extension of the domain of Mycenae beyond the confines of the Argive plain to a great part of the Peloponnesos. When Eurystheus was killed in a war against the children of Heracles and the Athenians, the people of Mycenae chose Atreus, the son of Pelops, to rule over them.

Atreus and his brother Thyestes came as refugees to Mycenae and to the court of Eurystheus who had married their sister. The jealousy between the two brothers culminated in the infamous love affair of Thyestes and the wife of Atreus and the abhorrent banquet prepared by the latter in which the two little children of Thyestes were served up to their father. When he had eaten and learned of the terrible deed Thyestes cried out an anguished curse which fell not on Atreus but on his children and his children's children. In spite of the atrocious crime, it seems that during Atreus' reign Mycenae's possessions were increased and consolidated and its importance was enhanced. Agamemnon, the son of Atreus, was chosen to lead the Achaean Greeks against Troy, the city of Priam, because, according to Thucydides, he was the most preeminent king in Greece. And we read in the Iliad that besides the plain of Argos he ruled over the territory of the northeastern section of the Peloponnesos, including Corinth, and he was also the "Lord of many isles".

The story of the Trojan War is well known. After the destruction of Troy Agamemnon returned victorious to Mycenae only to find death at the hands of his wife Klytemestra and her paramour Aegisthos, the youngest son of Thyestes. Their crime was not destined to remain unpunished, and so eight years later Orestes avenged the death of his father Agamemnon, by killing Aegisthos and Klytemestra. Tissamenos succeeded his father Orestes in the kingship of Mycenae and it was in his reign or shortly after it that Mycenae was captured and destroyed. Thucydides tells us that the destruction occurred eighty years after the fall of Troy, and at the hands of the Dorians, the last wave of Greek-speaking Indo-Europeans to establish themselves in the Peloponnesos. The final destruction put an end to the preeminence and leadership enjoyed by Mycenae for so long. That role was taken over by the Dorian cities of Corinth, Argos, and Sparta.

The misfortunes that befell the royal house of the Pelopids in fulfillment of Thyestes' curse were immortalized by the famous playwrights of Athens. The trilogy of Aeschylos known as the

Oresteia (Agamemnon-Choephoroi-Eumenides) is a most precious heirloom of our western world and a visitor to Mycenae must be sure to read at least the *Agamemnon*. On these tragedies are based T.S. Eliot's *The Family Reunion* (1939) and O'Neill's *Mourning Becomes Electra* (1932). It is almost impossible to determine the exact date of the legendary events mentioned. But the traditional genealogical accounts seem to indicate that Perseus was believed to have lived between 1400 and 1350 B.C.; Atreus around 1250 B.C.; Agamemnon around 1220 - 1190 B.C.; that, according to the prevailing tradition, the Trojan War was fought between 1200 - 1190 B.C. The final destruction of Mycenae of the Late Bronze Age was placed by tradition at the very end of the 12th century B.C.

That destruction did not entirely eliminate life. We read in Herodotos that when in 480 B.C. the Persian tide was rolling from the north and threatened to engulf Greece, the Mycenaean army stood with Leonidas' band at Thermopylae to stem it. From Thermopylae that army withdrew in obedience to the orders of the Spartans, but fought at the side of the Greeks against the Persians for the liberty of Greece at Plataea in 479 B.C. The victory of the Greeks and the liberation of their country from the invader filled the Mycenaeans with a new pride that provoked the jealousy of the people of Argos who did not participate in the war against the Persians. And so the Argives about 468 B.C. attacked Mycenae, forced its defenders to surrender and destroyed its citadel once more. Some 200 years later the Argives themselves rehabilitated the site, restored the fortifications where they were breached and ruined, and established a township that was active to the end of the pagan era. By then, decay had set in even in the township and when the traveler Pausanias visited the site towards the middle of the 2nd century of our era, he found but a few inhabitants and a good many ruins. H then saw, as he wrote, parts of the circuit wall with the Lion Gate, the underground " treasuries of Atreus and his children", the " graves of Agamemnon and those who were massacred with him on their return from

Troy" within the citadel, the graves of Aegisthos and Klytemestra beyond the walls (for they were not considered worthy to be buried within the citadel) and the Perseia fountain, among the ruins of Mycenae. Pausanias was the last of the ancient authors to mention our site. After him Mycenae passed into oblivion until late in the period of the Turkish occupation of Greece, towards the end of the 18th and the beginning of the 19th century of our era. Then it was noted by a number of early travelers and became the object of pilfering by art collectors and purveyors, Lord Sligo, Lord Elgin and Veli, the Pasha of Nafplion, being the better known despoilers of Mycenae. After the liberation of Greece, after 1833, such open depredations came to an end and the site came under the protection of the Greek Archaeological Society of Athens.

EXCAVATIONS

Mycenae, unlike Troy, was never completely covered, and its location, unlike that of Troy, was never subject to controversy. Throughout the ages its location was known to scholars and laymen alike and the stone lions guarding its entrance were always visible. Investigation of the site was started by the Greek Archaeological Society of Athens in 1840 when the clearing of the court before the Lion Gate was undertaken. Mycenae was dramatically brought to the attention of the world in 1876 when Heinrich Schliemann discovered and explored the royal cemetery of Mycenae, known now as Grave Circle A. His earlier attempt in 1874, lasting only five days in which 34 pits and trenches were dug, yielded remains that were not considered important by the explorer. But in the Grave Circle were preserved intact royal graves known as the shaft graves, filled with objects of gold, of silver, of bronze and of terracotta. The epic term " Mycenae rich in gold"received in 1876 a new and real meaning and its impressive citadel became the center of great activity.

72

In contrast to Schliemann who worked at Mycenae for 15 weeks only, the scholar who succeeded him in the exploration of the site, Chrestos Tsountas, labored for almost twenty years, from 1884 to 1902, with less glamorous but more important results. It was he who brought to light, among other things, the remains of the palace of Agamemnon, the subterranean cistern, the houses in the citadel, a good many chamber tombs which made possible the study of the burial customs of the Mycenaeans, and even some tholos tombs. In 1893 he published the earliest well-organized and reasoned account of the civilization whose fountainhead was proved to be Mycenae, and which came to be known as Mycenaean. The English version of the book by Ch. Tsountas and J. L. Manatt under the title *The Mycenaean Age* (Boston 1897), became one of the fundamental studies of the Late Bronze Age civilization of Greece.

After Tsountas, and for some 20 years, investigations of Mycenae remained in the background while Crete and the epoch-making discoveries of Sir Arthur Evans at Knossos dominated the scene of Greek archaeological research. Sporadic and minor investigations were undertaken by the late D. Evangelides (1909), G. Rodenwaldt (1911), and A. Keramopoullos (1917) but the effort to explore the famous site further was almost abandoned. Attention was directed again to Mycenae when the late Professor Alan J. B. Wace resumed large-scale investigations at the site in 1919 continuing to 1923. In the course of his excavations the remains in the citadel uncovered by Schliemann and Tsountas were further cleared and studied. New evidence was obtained that enabled Wace to draw a reasoned picture of the history and architectural phases of Mycenae, to give a clearer view of the successive periods of the culture developed there and more detailed definition of the burial customs of the period based on evidence yielded by a good number of graves he explored. In addition he re-examined the nine tholos tombs existing in the area of Mycenae, published the first complete study of their details and established the three successive stages of their construction.

His work, stopped temporarily in 1923, was resumed for a few weeks in 1939 but was interrupted by World War II. In 1950 Wace returned to the site and continued the exploration of the cemetery by the citadel and of the houses beyond it, until his death in 1957. The unfinished excavations which he left were completed by Mrs. A.J.B. Wace, by Mrs. David French and by Lord William Taylour with the final clearance of the so-called Citadel House taking place in the summer of 1969.

Meanwhile the Greek Archaeological Society of Athens resumed work at Mycenae and the Greek Service for the Restoration and Preservation of Ancient Monuments, under the direction first of Professor A.K. Orlandos and then of Dr. E. Stikas, in 1950 began work on the restoration of the so-called Tomb of Klytemestra, the palace on the summit and the Cyclopean walls of the citadel finishing in 1957. In the course of that work and in November 1951 the happy discovery of Grave Circle B was made, the second royal cemetery of Mycenae, some 120 meters west of the Lion Gate. The excavation of Grave Circle B by the late Dr. John Papadimitriou with an Advisory Committee composed of Professors A. Keramopoullos, Sp. Marinatos, and George E. Mylonas began in July 1952. In the first year all the members of the Committee participated in the work that revived the great days of the excavations of Mycenae and kindled anew the interest in the site. In 1953, 1954 the exploration of the Circle by Papadimitriou and Mylonas continued and was completed in 1955. The study of the Cyclopean walls and the gates of Mycenae followed, and also the excavation of the large West House by the late Ephor Nicolaos Verdeles, in the course of which a number of inscribed tablets were found, a welcome addition to those found previously by Wace in about the same area.

After the death of Wace and Papadimitriou (in the spring of 1963) the direction of the excavations at Mycenae were entrusted to George E. Mylonas and are continuing to the present under his direction.

RESULTS

As a result of the efforts of so many archaeologists representing so many parts of our Western civilized World, over a period of more than a century our knowledge of the life-history of Mycenae goes far beyond the traditions known to the Classical Greeks and even the knowledge of the mythographers of the ancient world. Indeed, we can maintain with reason that we know more about the beginnings of the life-history of Mycenae than Agamemnon knew when he was the king of that state. For we have seen that the legends go back only to Perseus who is assumed to have lived around 1400-1350 B.C. The work of the archaeologists takes us back to about 2500-2300 B.C., to the Early Bronze Age, when the site is proved to have been inhabited. Furthermore, it proved by the contents of the graves of the Grave Circles, that towards the end of the 17th and the beginning of the 16th century B.C. Mycenae was a state powerful, wealthy and preeminent in the affairs of mainland Greece.

However, legends and archaeological results agree in a number of points. In Homer Mycenae is called rich in gold; the excavation of the site brought to light more gold than that found in all the other Greek sites of all periods put together. Mycenae was known as the Cyclopean City; the walls of Mycenae fully revealed prove the title. Legends call it Broad-Wayed, the broad ramp leading to the palace from the Lion Gate and the roads radiating from the citadel prove that tradition was not wrong in awarding the title of Mycenae. Legends indicate that Mycenae was preeminent among the contemporary states of Greece; the remains uncovered establish its preeminence.

The type of art and culture revealed first by Schliemann and Tsountas came to be known as Mycenaean, since it was revealed at that site for the first time.

From those days to date similar art forms have been found in other parts of the Greek world and the term Mycenaean was broadened to include the entire Greek mainland of the Late

Bronze Age. And so when we say Mycenaean civilization we mean not only that developed at Mycenae but also in the rest of Greece between the years ca. 1620 to 1120 B.C. Also the term «Mycenaeans» is applied to the population of the mainland Greece of the Late Bronze Age and not only to the people of Mycenae. The beginnings of the Mycenaean Age are placed in the times when the local culture of the Greek-speaking Indo-Europeans, who were already established in the mainland of Greece by 1900 B.C., came under the all pervading influence of Minoan art and culture and gradually developed into the art represented by the finds in the royal shaft graves of Grave Circles A and B. That influence continued to be strong for a good many years and to about 1450 B.C. when the Mycenaean culture developed on different original lines.

That date marks the period of greatest expansion and influence of the Mycenaeans in both the Eastern and the Western Mediterranean area. Their merchants carried the products of the homeland—olive oil, perfumed oils, wine, works of art and pottery—to Egypt, Palestine and Syria, to the west coast of Asia Minor and its adjacent islands of Rhodes and Samos, to Southern Italy and Sicily and perhaps as far west as South Wales where on one of the pillars of the outer circle at Stonehenge lately was observed incised a Mycenaean dagger. In exchange they brought home, copper, gold, tin, ivory, aromatic herbs and cultural and artistic ideas. They first established trading stations and then veritable colonies in a number of islands, often subduing and replacing flourishing Minoan stations. Taking advantage of the devastating volcanic eruption of Thera and a violent earthquake that destroyed the Cretan palaces around 1475 B.C., the Mycenaeans conquered Knossos, and established themselves in the very capital of Minos from where they ruled perhaps over a good part of Crete itself for a number of generations.

The 14th and the 13th centuries B.C. continued to be periods of prosperity and expansion. It was then that a number of citadels were surrounded by Cyclopean walls and a number of imposing

Fig. 31. Temple Γ. The horseshoe-shaped altar is covered with earth for preservation, but the slaughtering stone can be seen easily.

palaces were erected in various parts of the mainland of Greece. Then were constructed the most monumental tholos tombs at Mycenaé — the «Treasury of Atreus» and the «Tomb of Klytemestra» — and at Orchomenos — the «Treasury of Minyas». The political system of the city states ruled over by a king, known as a *wanax* (the Homeric *anax*) was developed and crystalized, and a bureaucratic hierarchy and control was established in a number of states, at least at Pylos and Knossos. In those two places hundreds of clay tablets were found inscribed in Linear B script, telling us of the possessions of the *wanax* and offering a glimpse into the political system, the land tenure, the religion and the division of people in guilds and classes. They also indicate that

77

although the Mycenaeans were warriors and merchants, they did not neglect the land, that they were good agriculturalists and tenders and raisers of animals. They grew wheat and millet, tended olive trees and orchards which yielded figs, almonds, walnuts and cherries. Cattle did not seem to be plentiful, but sheep and goats and swine were common. Horses, too, were valued and raised and the plain of Argos was known in Homeric times as the «horse-breeding» plain.

It seems probable that Linear B script was developed from the earlier Minoan Linear A script when the Mycenaeans occupied Knossos and had to have a record of all the revenues of the state. The earlier script did not possess signs for certain syllabic sounds common to the Greek language; so new signs had to be added to its syllabary to make possible the recording if inventories in the language of the conqueror—Mycenaeans which differed from the Minoan. For a long time Linear B script defied decipherment; but in the fifties Michael Ventris specified syllabic values to the signs of the script and, with the help of John Chadwick, was able to read and interpret a number of inscriptions or tablets. The effort to read and interpret the documents in Linear B script developed into an almost separate branch of archaeology (often referred to as Mycenology) and scholars the world over are now engaged in the study. Many problems connected with the decipherment are still to be solved, but Ventris' monumental contribution has established a solid basis on which to build and beyond which it is possible now to extend. Another major result of Ventris' work is the proof that the language of Linear B script is Greek, that the Mycenaeans were Greek-speaking people.

Thus far at Mycenae some 68 fragments and tablets were found, and here we do not seem to have the extreme control of the activities of the citizenry by the *wanax* and the elaborate bureaucracy that appears to have existed at Pylos and Knossos. Nevertheless in Mycenae, too, the king, the *wanax,* was in supreme control and a section of his palace served the artists and artisans who produced so many of the articles that illustrate the Mycenaean culture and which were exported.

It seems that in the second half of the 13th century a number of disasters overtook the realm of Mycenae. Houses were destroyed by fire, areas were abandoned, even the palace, or part of it, was burned down. The greatest destruction seems to have occurred shortly after 1200 B.C. It was then that the palace was burned again and a number of buildings within and without the citadel were destroyed by fire. Scholars disagree as to the cause of these destructions at Mycenae, that seem to be paralleled by destruction in other sites of the Mycenaean world. Some believe that the second half of the 13th century was a period of peril and the beginning of the decay of the Mycenaean power and culture. And yet in that half of the century a number of imposing monuments were erected at Mycenae: the Lion Gate with its monumental relief proving self-confidence, pride and prosperity, the «Treasury of Atreus» and the «Tomb of Klytemestra», the most imposing structures of the prehistoric world, to mention but a few. Ivory continued to flow to Mycenae from Syria proving that the commercial activities of the Mycenaeans were not severed. And after 1200 B.C. there is a notable effort on the part of the people of Mycenae, who continued to live within their high walls, to recuperate from the disasters of that date, to rebuild their fortunes. This, I believe, can only be explained by the misfortunes that befell to the ruling family of Mycenae after the termination of the Trojan War.

The date of the fall of Troy is not definitely established with unanimity. It seems to us that the city of Priam was destroyed by the Achaean-Greeks (by the Mycenaeans) around 1200 B.C. It was then that Agamemnon, the supreme commander of the Achaeans, was slaughtered and, as we have seen above, shortly afterwards his murderers were killed by Orestes, the son of Agamemnon.

It is natural to assume that those violent deeds within the royal family disrupted life, destroyed the prestige of the *wanax,* and created factions, internal struggle for power, and disunity. This resulted in destruction of buildings within and without the citadel; in the breaking of law and order in the country; people fled from their exposed villages and towns to places of safety beyond the domain of the feuding factions. This disrupted commercial activities always initiated by the strong and the ambitious who were now engaged in internal struggle, and reduced the prosperity and the cultural activities of the people. This, I believe, will explain the disasters of ca. 1200 B.C. and the efforts for recuperation that followed since after a while peace must have been established among the feuding parties and the Mycenaeans must have tried to revive their old activities. It can be proved that they continued to occupy their citadel. But this recuperation was not brought to a successful peak because then the area of Mycenae was infiltrated by bands of invaders known as the Dorians, who taking advantage of the weakness of the state, brought about by internal disunity, kept attacking the villages in the country. Gradually moving southward over the years, finally ca. 1120 B.C. these bands of Dorians managed to deliver the *coup de grâce* to Mycenae by taking its citadel and destroying its palaces and houses completely. This destruction brought to an end the leadership which Mycenae exercised for centuries and put an end to its preeminence in cultural and political matters. As we have seen, Mycenaeans survived the disaster and continued to live in the old site down through the years of the historic era of Greece, but now Mycenae was transformed into an insignificant village which only in the days of the Persian invasion of Greece, in 480 B.C., experienced a shortlived period of glory. However, the culture developed on its hills in the Heroic Age provided the leven from which rose the Classical achievement of Greece that forms the solid foundation of our Western civilization.